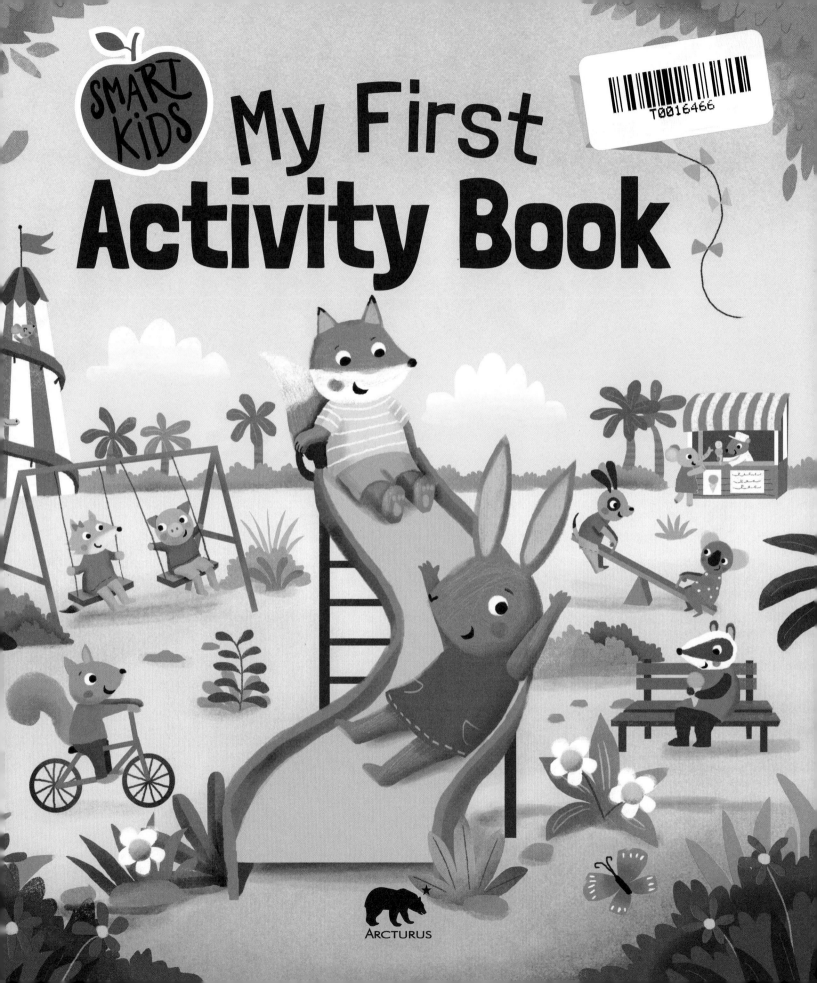

SMART KIDS
My First Activity Book

ARCTURUS

ARCTURUS

This edition published in 2023 by Arcturus Publishing Limited
26/27 Bickels Yard, 151–153 Bermondsey Street,
London SE1 3HA

Author: Lisa Regan
Illustrator: Kate Daubney
Editor: Violet Peto
Designer: Nathan Balsom
Managing Editor: Joe Harris
Design Manager: Jessica Holliland

ISBN: 978-1-3988-2560-4
CH010452NT
Supplier 29, Date 1122, PI 00002449

Printed in China

Apples and Pears

Charlie Bear loves apples. Missy Bear loves pears.
Who gets the most of the fruit they like best?

Hocus Pocus

Welcome to Magical Merlin's school for wizards!
See if you can find all of the spellbinding items from the list.

Tasty Treats

Which of Rumiko Rabbit's delicious ice cream sundaes isn't quite the same as the others?

Look Outside

What has landed outside Stephanie's window?
Connect the dots to find out!

Something Missing

Yikes! These vehicles each have a wheel missing!
Look carefully to see which wheel
should go back on each vehicle.

A Walk in the Park

Tansy Turtle loves to walk in the sunshine. Guide her from the green gate to the blue gate, so she can enjoy all the sights.

START

FINISH

Brush, Brush, Brush!

Which of these clever crocodiles has the most teeth?
Look how clean and shiny their teeth are!

Mrs. Hop's Flowers

What a beautiful display! Draw more petals,
so that each flower has 10 petals.

Listen to the Band

What a beautiful sound they make!
Which of the tiles isn't part of the main picture?

Pretty as a Picture

Which of the pretty peacocks is a tiny bit different from the others?

Memory Test

Study this school photo, and then turn the page
to see which students have swapped places.

Memory Test

Can you remember who was sitting where? Then see who has swapped places.

Puppy Training

Which of the puppies walks nicely and makes it all the way to the cones at the end?

On the Seashore

Which of Sophie Bunny's seashells needs to go in each space to finish each pattern?

Matchmaking

Find each pair of fish, and use pens or crayons to
make the black and white ones match their partners.

Lots of Lemurs!

Which of the silhouette shapes matches the lemur in the middle?

ID Parade

These guys are having a great time! See if you can find all these penguins in the picture:

A penguin on
skates

A penguin with
a red beak

A penguin wearing
green glasses

Tiger Twins

Which two tigers are the same?

Hiding in the Jungle

The names of three jungle birds are hidden in these letters.
Can you find them? Cross out all of the other letters.

GRPARROTHBTOUCANWREAGLEKH

Time for a Change

Match each caterpillar to the butterfly it will
turn into. Use the patterns to help you.

Feeling Good

Mrs. Hop is feeling happy today!
Can you find the word HAPPY
hidden just once in the grid?

```
H  P  A  P  P  P  Y  H
H  P  A  Y  P  A  P  Y
P  A  H  P  A  H  Y  Y
Y  A  P  P  Y  H  A  P
P  H  Y  A  P  P  H  A
H  A  H  A  P  P  Y  P
A  P  P  Y  H  A  P  Y
P  A  H  Y  P  P  Y  H
```

Magpie Treasures

Find a way through the jewels following them in this order.
You can move across and down, but not diagonally.

START

FINISH

Eggs-actly!

How many ostrich eggs can you count?
Are there the same number of eggs as there are ostriches?

In the Jungle

Study the jungle scene, then decide whether each of the sentences below is true or false.

The toucan is sitting on a branch.

The frog is red with black spots.

The blue butterfly is bigger than the yellow one.

There is a snake on the highest branch.

There are no orange flowers.

Jump for Joy

Which three pieces are needed to finish the puzzle?

A   B   C   D   E

Hustle and Bustle

Look at the two pictures below. Which two animals have left the airport in the second scene?

Driving Around

How is Sally Sheep getting into town? Connect the dots to find out!

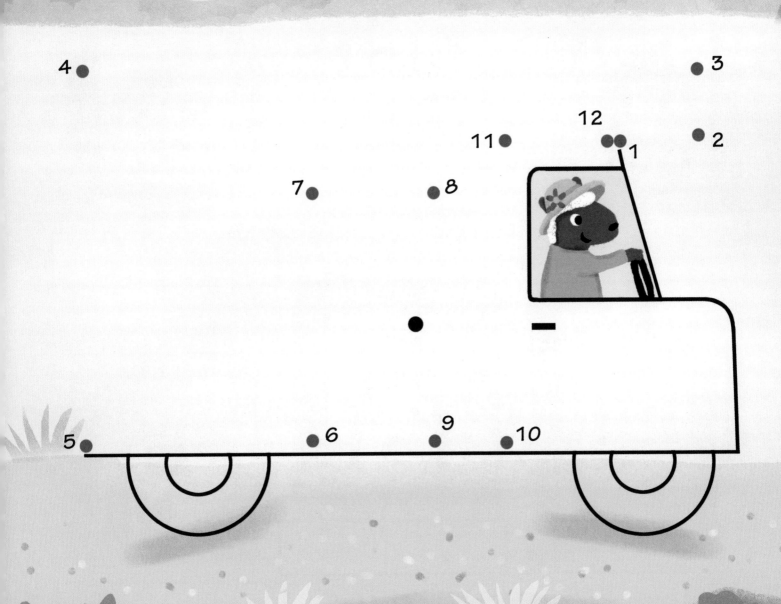

Who's Who?

Write the correct name beneath each of the pictures.

- The horse is named Harry.
- Hugo has long, floppy ears.
- Hermione is black and white.
- Hector is a prickly character.
- The owl is named Huong.
- Himani is wearing a hat.

Going Underground

Help Pico Pig through the cave
to find the magnificent waterfall.

START

FINISH

I Can Count

Which are there more of, big black-and-white fish
or small black-and-white fish? Count them to find out!

Dressing Up

Finish the costumes by adding a hat and accessories,
and then use your crayons to liven things up.

Fun in the Sun

Oh, we do like to be beside the seaside!
Find each of the items that are shown on the side.

Toy Trucks

Which of Ricky Raccoon's trucks is a tiny bit different from the others?

Time for a Trim

Troy the hairdresser is ready for his next client! The names of three items he uses are hidden in these letters. Can you find them? Cross out all of the other letters.

Picnic in the Park

Kayla Koala has brought sandwiches to the picnic, and Bobby Badger
has brought donuts. Who brought the most treats?

Catch of the Day

Which of the friends has managed to catch a fish?
Follow the lines to find out.

Beautiful Beads

Which of the scattered beads needs to go in each space to finish the pattern on the necklace?

You Try!

Use the grid lines to help you copy the picture into the blank space.

Flying High

Up, up, and away! Which of the tiles isn't part of the main picture?

Market Day

It's very busy in the market today.
Can you spot six differences between the two pictures?

Memory Test

It's party time! Check out who's here,
and then turn the page to see who has swapped partners.

Memory Test

Can you remember who was dancing together and see who has swapped partners?

A Whale of a Time!

Can you find the word WHALE
hidden in the grid three times?

```
W A L E H L E A
H E W H A L E W
E W E A W H A H
A H L W H E A A
L A E H H W H L
E L W E A L H L
W E H L W H A E
W H A L E L H E
```

Traffic Jam

Find a way through the cars following them in this order.
You can move across and down, but not diagonally.

START

FINISH

My Marbles!

Tansy is collecting green marbles.
Tony is collecting yellow marbles. Who can collect the most?

A Shady Character

Which of the silhouette shapes matches the sly fox in the middle?

Puppy Parade

Which of the dogs is the same as the one in the photograph?

Turtley Different

All of these turtles are different, apart from a pair of twins.
Can you spot the two that look the same?

54

From Me to You

What present does Charlie Bear have for Missy Bear? Connect the dots to find out!

Heading for Home

Each bug lives in a house that coordinates with its hat and boots.
Which bug doesn't live on this street?

As Fast as a Fox

Fernando Fox is in a hurry! Help him drive from the forest to the stores before they close for the night.

START

FINISH

Taking Stock

Magical Merlin has made lots of potions! Help him count them,
and write the numbers on his stock list at the bottom.

A Lovely Lunch

What would you have for lunch if you could choose anything? Draw it here!

A Big Day Out

Study the beach scene, and then decide whether each of the sentences below is true or false.

- The surfers are all standing up.

- The gull is eating a sandwich.

- None of the crabs is red.

- The pink shell is bigger than the others.

- The blue-and-white beach ball is in the water.

Baking Buddies

Which three pieces are needed to finish the puzzle?

A   B   C   D   E

Not That Knit

Stephanie Stork has knitted scarves for all her friends.
Which one of them is a tiny bit different?

Memory Test

Study this crowd, and then turn the page
to see which fans have swapped places.

Memory Test

Can you remember who was sitting where and see who has swapped places?

Trash Raiders

Follow the wiggly lines to see who has made such a mess!

Planning Ahead

Rumiko Rabbit uses the same ingredients to make her world-famous pasta sauce. Which of the sets of ingredients is wrong?

Mix or Match?

Use the top picture and copy it with your pens and crayons—
or if you prefer, do your own thing and make it completely different!

The Great Outdoors

Gracie Goat is very busy! Find each of the items that are shown on the side.

Happy Times

Look at the two scenes below. Which two animals have left the picnic in the second scene? Which two have joined the friends?

Big Cat Quest

The names of three big cats are hidden in these letters.
Can you find them? Cross out all of the other letters.

ALIONRYTIGERMELEOPARDP

I See Seahorses

Can you find a blue seahorse with green markings
swimming among the seaweed?

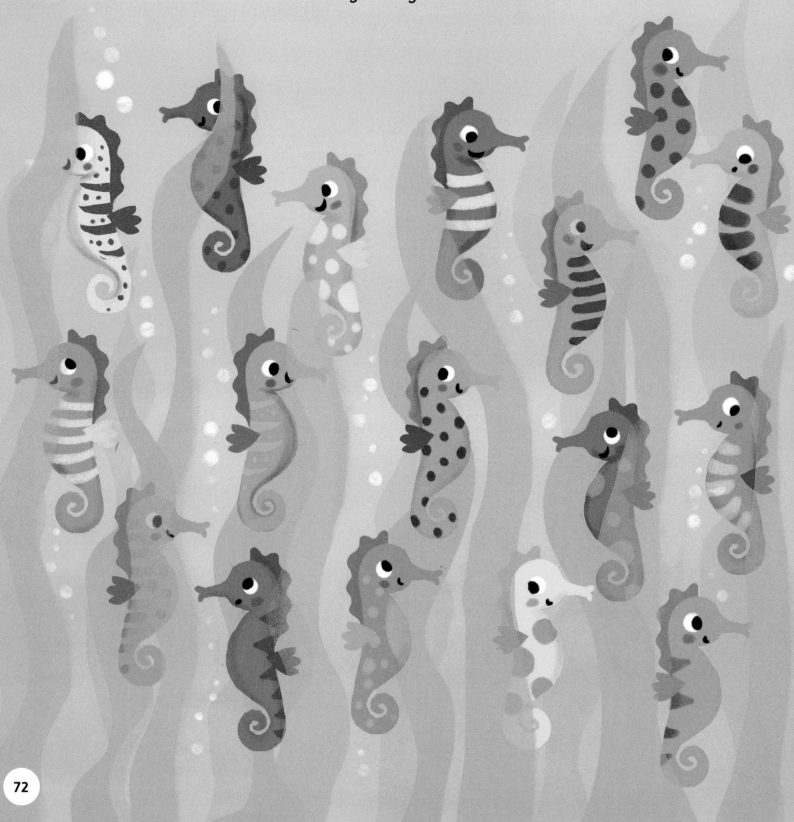

In the Trees

Can you find all the tree-dwelling animals written in the grid?
BAT, FROG, LEMUR, OWL, PARROT, ROBIN, SLOTH, SNAKE

F	R	R	A	L	S	G	T
S	N	A	K	E	L	A	L
F	P	A	R	R	O	T	E
R	L	S	B	H	T	W	M
O	E	B	H	T	H	I	U
B	T	A	W	O	W	L	R
I	N	T	O	I	U	K	O
N	D	S	F	R	O	G	B

Shell Seekers

Help Tansy Turtle find these four
shells in a row on the beach.

Snack Time

Ricky Raccoon eats all the cherries. Rocco Raccoon eats all the strawberries.
Who eats the most?

Ahoy There!

Look carefully at Bruno's pirate map.
Which of the small squares isn't actually from the map?

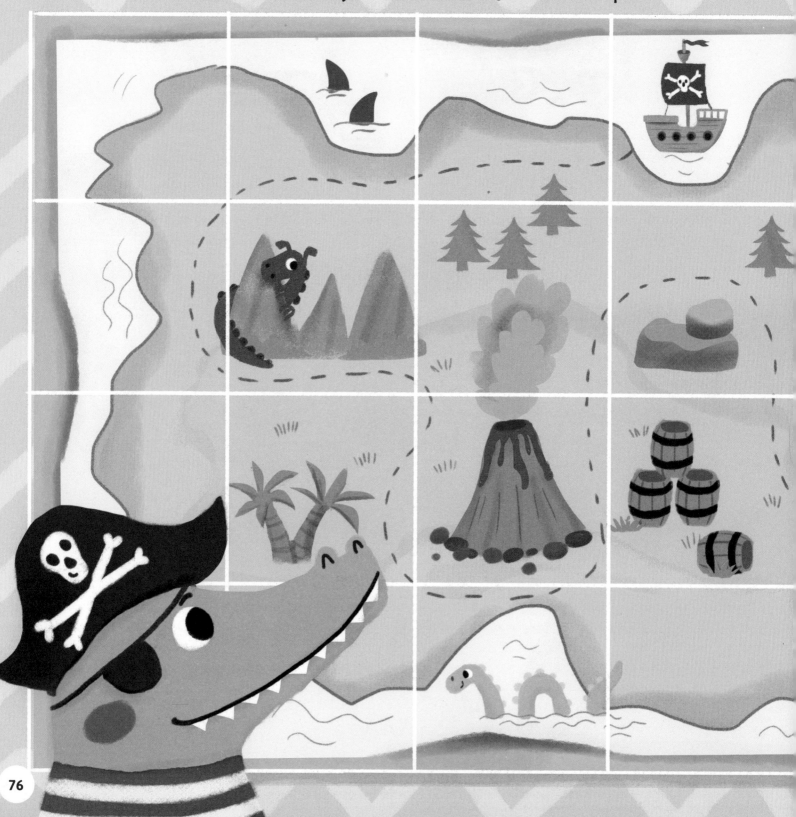

Ready, Set, Go!

Look carefully at these two pictures, and
try to find six differences between them.

Party Piece

Felicity Fox is nearly ready for her party guests to arrive.
What is the one thing she still needs to find? Connect the dots to see what it is!

Feathered Friends

Write the correct name beneath each of the pictures.

- The black bird is named Mercedes.
- Mila is black and white.
- The bird with the biggest beak is Matteo.

- Miles is red and blue.
- Max is wearing a bow tie.
- Maria has a balloon.

Ding-a-Ling

Which string should Suki Sea Lion
pull to ring the bell?

Shooting Stars

Benson and Belinda are stargazing. How many shooting stars can you count in the sky?

Finish These Faces!

Can you add some eyes, ears, and whiskers to these cute creatures?

Answers

Page 3

There are six pears and four apples, so Missy Bear gets most of the fruit she likes.

Pages 4–5

Page 6

Page 7

Page 8

Page 9

Page 10

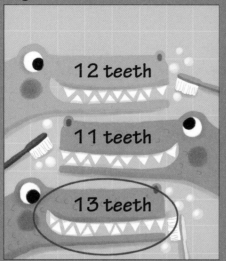

12 teeth

11 teeth

13 teeth

Page 11

Pages 12–13

Page 14

Page 15

Page 16

These students have swapped places: Hippo and Bear; Tiger and Lemur.

Page 17

Page 18

Page 19

Page 20

Page 21

- A penguin wearing green glasses
- A penguin on skates
- A penguin with a red beak

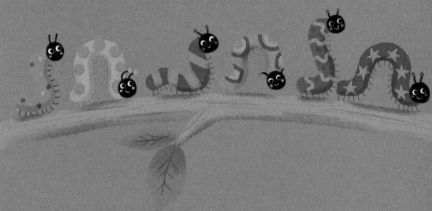

Page 22

Page 23

G̶R̶PARROTH̶B̶TOUCANW̶R̶EAGLEK̶H̶

Page 24

Page 25

Page 26

Page 27

No, there are not the same number of eggs and ostriches. There are four eggs, and there are five ostriches.

Page 28

- The toucan is sitting on a branch. TRUE
- The frog is red with black spots. FALSE—The frog is yellow with black spots
- The blue butterfly is bigger than the yellow one. FALSE—The yellow butterfly is bigger than the blue one.
- There is a snake on the highest branch. TRUE
- There are no orange flowers. TRUE

Page 29

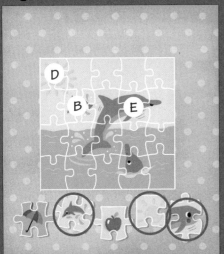

Page 30

Elephant and Badger have left the airport. Tiger and Dog have arrived at the airport.

Page 31

Page 32

HUONG

HERMIONE

HIMANI

HUGO

HECTOR

HARRY

Page 33

Page 34

There are five big black-and-white fish, and there are six small black-and-white fish. Therefore, there are more small black-and-white fish than there are big black-and-white fish.

Pages 36–37

Page 38

Page 39

O̶O̶SCISSORST̶G̶BRUSHL̶I̶SHAMPOOV̶

Page 40

Kayla Koala brought seven sandwiches, and Bobby Badger brought six donuts, so Kayla Koala brought the most treats.

Page 41

Page 42

Pages 44–45

Page 46

Page 47

Page 48

These dance partners
have swapped places:
Pig and Deer.

Page 49

Page 50

Page 51

Tansy can collect seven green marbles, and Tony can collect nine yellow marbles, so Tony can collect the most.

Page 52

Page 53

Page 54

Page 55

Page 56

Page 57

Page 58

Page 60

- The surfers are all standing up. FALSE—One surfer is lying down.
- The gull is eating a sandwich. FALSE—The gull is eating a fish.
- None of the crabs is red. TRUE

- The pink shell is bigger than the others. FALSE—The pink shell is smaller than the others.
- The blue-and-white beach ball is in the water. FALSE—It is on a towel.

Page 61

Page 62

Page 63

Page 64

These sports fans have swapped places:
Frog and Lemur;
Cat and Dog.

Page 65

Page 66

Pages 68–69

Page 70

Panda and Frog have left the picnic—Horse and Squirrel have joined.

Page 71

ALIONRYTIGERMELEOPARDP

Page 72

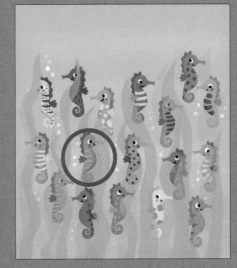

Page 73

Page 74

Page 75

There are 16 cherries and 13 strawberries, so Ricky Raccoon eats the most.

Page 76–77

Page 78

Page 79

Page 80

MAX
MILA
MARIA
MERCEDES
MILES
MATTEO

Page 81

Page 82

There are 12 shooting stars.